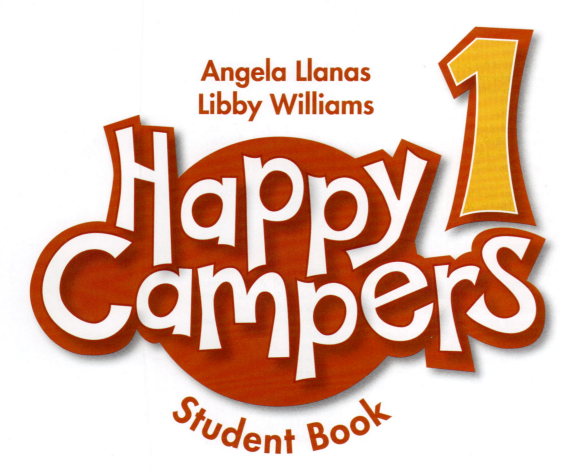

Macmillan Education
4 Crinan Street
London N1 9XW
A division of Macmillan Publishers Limited

Companies and representatives throughout the world

ISBN 9788551102022

Text, design and illustration © Macmillan Publishers Limited 2015
Written by Angela Llanas and Libby Williams
The authors have asserted their rights to be identified as the authors of this work in accordance with the Copyright, Designs and Patents Act 1988.

Happy Campers is a registered trademark, property of HM Publishers Holdings Limited

First published 2015

All rights reserved; no part of this publication may be reproduced, stored in a retrieval system, transmitted in any form, or by any means, electronic, mechanical, photocopying, recording, or otherwise, without the prior written permission of the publishers.

Designed by Pronk Media Inc.
Student Book pages illustrated by: Luciana Navarro Powell (stories: pp. 12–13, 20–21, 36, 44); Pronk Media Inc. (pp. 8–9, 10, 15, 16–17, 18, 21, 23, 24–25, 26–27, 31, 32–33, 34, 37, 39, 40–41, 42, 47, 48–49, 50, 52–53, 55, 56–57, 63, 64–65, 66, 69, 71, 72); Paul Sharp (comic strips: pp. 6–7, 10–11, 18–19, 26–27, 34–35, 42–43, 50–51, 58–59, 66–67)
The Language Lodge pages illustrated by: Pronk Media Inc. (pp. 1, 3, 5, 6–7, 8–9, 10–11, 12–13, 14–15, 16–17, 18–19, 20–21, 22–23, 24–25, 27, 28–29, 30–31, 32)
Cover design and illustration by Roberto Martínez
Cover photograph by George Contorakes
Picture research by Penelope Bowden, Proudfoot Pictures

The authors and publishers would like to thank the following for permission to reproduce their photographs: **Alamy**/Anyka p. 49(t), Alamy/Redmund Durrell p. 48(br), Alamy/Eureka p. 41(cl), Alamy/Gina Kelly p. 41(tl); **Brandx** pp. 32(br), 48(tr,mr), 64(tr); **Comstock Images** pp. 64(cr), 65(bl); **Corbis**/Rick Gayl p. 33(t), Corbis/Frank Lukasseck p. 25(b), Corbis/ILYA NAYMUSHIN/Reuters pp. 68(tr), 69(l), Corbis/Ocean pp. 60(br), 61(mr); **Digital Vision** pp. 28(tr), 29(cl); **Getty Images** p. 64(tl), Getty Images/Augustus Butera p. 24(b), Getty Images/Jeff R Clow pp. 68(mr), 69(cr), Getty Images/Danita Delimont pp. 28(tl), 29(b), Getty Images/Digital Vision pp. 68(bl), 69(r), Getty Images/Christian Heeb p. 41(tc,mr), Getty Images/Jostein Nilsen Photography pp. 40(l), 41(tr); **Macmillan Publishers Ltd.**/Paul Bricknell pp. 32(t), 33(bl); **Nature Picture Library**/Markus Varesvuo pp. 28(br), 29(t); **Photodisc** p. 24(t), PhotoDisc/Getty Images pp. 65(br), 68(tl), 69(cl); **Superstock**/Juniors pp. 28(bl), 29(cr), Superstock/Sheltered Images pp. 60(tr), 61(t); **Thinkstock** pp. 25(t), 65(tl), Thinkstock/Akabei pp. 60(tl), 61(ml), Thinkstock/Cynoclub p. 41(bl,br), Thinkstock/Jupiterimages pp. 60(bl), 61(b), Thinkstock/Debra Millet p. 49(b), Thinkstock/Jim Pruitt p. 57(t); **Up the Resolution** p. 68(br)

Commissioned photographs by George Contorakes, pp. 8–9, 14, 16–17, 22, 30, 32–33, 38, 46, 48, 54, 57, 62, 64–65, 70

The authors and publishers wish to thank the following for their help with the photo shoot: Karen Greer Models, LLC; Chloe; Christian; Christopher; and Zoey

These materials may contain links for third party websites. We have no control over, and are not responsible for, the contents of such third party websites. Please use care when accessing them.

Contents

Student Book

Scope and Sequence............................4
Welcome......................................6
Unit 1..8
Unit 2.......................................16
Unit 3.......................................24
Unit 4.......................................32
Unit 5.......................................40
Unit 6.......................................48
Unit 7.......................................56
Unit 8.......................................64
Word Play!...................................72

The Language Lodge

Unit 1..1
Unit 2..5
Unit 3..9
Unit 4.......................................13
Unit 5.......................................17
Unit 6.......................................21
Unit 7.......................................25
Unit 8.......................................29

Scope and Sequence

Unit	Pages	Vocabulary	Grammar
1	8–15	**Greetings:** hello, hi, goodbye, bye **Family:** mom, dad, sister, grandma, grandpa, brother	What's your name? My name's Amy. This is my brother.
2	16–23	**Numbers:** 1–10 **School Supplies:** pencil, pen, ruler, eraser, crayon, colored pencil	How old are you? I'm seven. I have a pencil. I have an eraser.
3	24–31	**Animals:** cat, dog, opossum, horse, alligator, rabbit **Forest Animals:** bear, fox, deer, owl, snake, eagle	What is it? It's an alligator. It's a cat. It isn't an owl.
4	32–39	**Toys:** doll, truck, kite, ball, yo-yo, teddy bear **Colors:** red, green, yellow, blue, black, white	Is it a doll? Yes, it is. / No, it isn't. What color is it? It's red.
5	40–47	**Parts of a Room:** window, floor, table, chair, door, wall **Hiking:** map, water bottle, snack, backpack, towel, hat	The cat is under the table. The ball is in the box. Where's my backpack? It's on the chair.
6	48–55	**Nature:** tree, plant, butterfly, caterpillar, frog, ladybug **Colors:** gray, purple, orange, brown, pink, beige	What are they? They're trees. They aren't pink. Are they brown? Yes, they are.
7	56–63	**Parts of the House:** kitchen, living room, dining room, bedroom, bathroom, yard **Numbers:** 11–20	There is one kitchen. There are three bedrooms. How many bathrooms are there?
8	64–71	**Food:** hamburger, hot dog, pizza, French fries, milk, cookie **Fruits and Vegetables:** peas, apple, orange, banana, carrot, tomato	I like hamburgers. I don't like peas.

Extra Practice	Teamwork Activity
The Language Lodge: Pages 1–4 **Happy Campers app:** Unit 1	Family Memory
The Language Lodge: Pages 5–8 **Happy Campers app:** Unit 2	School Time Puzzle
The Language Lodge: Pages 9–12 **Happy Campers app:** Unit 3	Animal Bingo
The Language Lodge: Pages 13–16 **Happy Campers app:** Unit 4	Five Questions
The Language Lodge: Pages 17–20 **Happy Campers app:** Unit 5	Find It
The Language Lodge: Pages 21–24 **Happy Campers app:** Unit 6	Ask Me
The Language Lodge: Pages 25–28 **Happy Campers app:** Unit 7	My Mansion
The Language Lodge: Pages 29–32 **Happy Campers app:** Unit 8	Lunchtime Memory

UNIT 1 Lesson 1

1 Listen. Then echo.

Hello.

Hi.

Goodbye.

Bye.

2 Listen and point.

Hello! 🎵

Hello! Hi!
What's your name?

My name's Mike.

Mike

Lisa

3   The Language Lodge

Lesson 2

1   Sing: **Hello!**

2 **Grammar Check! Complete.**

1. What's _____ name?

   _____ name's Mike.

2. _____ your _____?

   _____ _____ Katie.

Goodbye! Goodbye! Bye! Bye! Bye!

Katie

Dan

3 **Point, ask, and answer.**

Hi. What's your name?

Hello. My name's Sara.

4   **The Language Lodge**

Lesson 3

1   **Read and listen.**

2 **Find and complete. Then listen and say.**

1. __ o m
2. __ a d
3. __ i s t e r
4. __ r a n d m a
5. __ r a n d p a
6. __ r o t h e r

3   **The Language Lodge**

10

Lesson 4

1 06 **Listen again to Happy Camp.**

2 **Grammar Check! Circle.**

1. This is my brother / dad.
2. This is my mom / grandma.
3. This is my sister / grandpa.

3 08 **Listen and cheer!**

This is my grandma. Hello, Grandma!
This is my grandpa. Hi, Grandpa!

4 **The Language Lodge**

Lesson 5

1   **Read and listen.**

The Happy Kite

I'm Twig.
This is my sister Daisy.
Look, Daisy! A kite!

This is my brother Root.
Hey, Root! Look! A kite!

Hello, Mom and Dad!
Hello, Grandma and Grandpa!
This is my kite.

Goodbye!

Lesson 6

1 09 **Listen again to The Happy Kite.**

2 **Complete. Then number the family members.**

1. s ister
2. ___ rother
3. ___ om
4. ___ ad
5. ___ randma
6. ___ randpa

Lesson 7
Make and Play!

1 **Make** family picture cards.

2 **Play** Family Memory!

This is mom.

Yes!

Lesson 8

1 🐝 **Spelling!** Match.

1. hel — lo
2. good — bye
3. h — i
4. b — ye

2 Circle six family words. Match.

g	r	a	n	d	p	a
m	s	i	s	t	e	r
o	d	r	e	d	a	d
g	r	a	n	d	m	a
h	a	d	i	r	t	h
e	n	m	o	m	d	p
b	r	o	t	h	e	r

3 **Word Play!** Find and circle the words from Unit 1 on Page 72.

UNIT 2   Lesson 1

1 🐶 10

Listen. Then echo.

1 one
2 two
3 three
4 four
5 five
6 six
7 seven
8 eight
9 nine
10 ten

2 🐶 11 Listen and draw candles.

Counting Song

How old are you?
How old are you?
Count with me,
And you can see!
I'm one, two, three,
Four, five, six, seven!
I am seven!

3 🏠 Page 5   The Language Lodge

16

Lesson 2

1 🐶 11 **Sing: Counting Song.**

2 **Grammar Check!** Complete and answer for Lisa.

How _____ are _____?

I'm _____.

3 Ask and answer.

4   **The Language Lodge**

Lesson 3

1   **Read and listen.**

2   **Find and complete. Then listen and say.**

1. p encil
2. ___ en
3. ___ uler
4. ___ raser
5. ___ rayon
6. ___ olored pencil

3   **The Language Lodge**

Lesson 4

1 **Listen again to Happy Camp.**

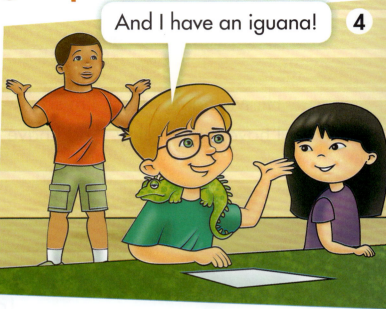

2 **Grammar Check!** **Match.**

1. I have an eraser.
2. I have a ruler.
3. I have an iguana.
4. I have crayons.

3 **Listen and cheer!**

I have a pencil. Yeah!
I have an eraser. Yeah!

CHEER BOX!

4 **The Language Lodge**

Lesson 5

1   **Read and listen.**

Carl's Idea

Hi. My name's Carl. I'm six.
I have a lot of clay. And I have an idea!

Look! Now I have a pencil,
an eraser, and a ruler.

I have a pencil, an eraser,
and a ruler.
And now I have two crayons!

Mom! Look at my clay school supplies!
Oh, no!

Lesson 6

1 Listen again to Carl's Idea.

2 Circle.

1. Carl is seven.   Yes   (No)
2. Carl has a pencil.   Yes   No
3. Carl has a pen.   Yes   No
4. Carl has an eraser.   Yes   No

3 Check (✓) the problem with Carl's school supplies.

1. ☐

2. ☐

3. ☐

21

Lesson 7
Make and Play!

1 **Make** a school supplies puzzle.

2 **Play** School Time Puzzle!

Look! I have a crayon!

Yes!

Lesson 8

1 **Spelling!** Count aloud and complete.

1. ___ i ___ e

2. ___ o u ___

3. ___ ___ n e

2 Draw school supplies. Then complete.

1. I have _____ _____ .

2. I have _____ _____ .

3 **Word Play!** Find and circle the words from Unit 2 on Page 72.

23

UNIT 3 Lesson 1

1 Listen. Then echo.

cat

dog

opossum

horse

alligator

rabbit

2 Listen and number.

My Fun Pet!

What is it?
It's my pet.

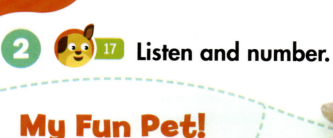

☐ It's a dog.
Yes, you bet!

☐ It's an alligator.
Yes, you bet!

3 Page 9 **The Language Lodge**

Lesson 2

1 🐶 17 **Sing:**
My Fun Pet!

1 It's a cat.
   Yes, you bet!

   It's an opossum.
   Yes, you bet!

2 Grammar Check! Match.

It's — a — alligator.
      an cat.
          dog.
          opossum.

3 Point, ask, and answer.

What is it? It's a dog.

4 🏠 Page 10 **The Language Lodge**

25

Lesson 3

1   Read and listen.

2 Find and complete. Then listen and say.

1. <u>b</u> e a r
2. ___ o x
3. ___ e e r
4. ___ w l
5. ___ n a k e
6. ___ a g l e

3 The Language Lodge

Lesson 4

1 🐶 18 **Listen again to Happy Camp.**

2 **Grammar Check!** Match.

1. 🦉 It's an eagle.
2. 🦊 It isn't a bear.
3. 🐍 It's a snake.
4. 🦌 It's a horse.

True

False

3 🐶 20 **Listen and cheer!**

It's a fox. It's a fox. Yes! Yes! Yes!
It isn't a bear. No! No! No!

CHEER BOX!

4 🏠 Page 12 **The Language Lodge**

Lesson 5

1   **Read and listen.**

Wild Animals

What is it?
An owl?
No, it isn't an owl. It's an eagle.

Look! It's a bear.
It's a brown bear.

Look at the fox.
It's beautiful!

What is it?
A deer?
No, it isn't a deer. It's a horse.

Lesson 6

1 **Listen again to Wild Animals.**

2 Match.

1. It isn't an owl.

2. It's brown.

3. It isn't a deer.

4. It's beautiful.

Lesson 7
Make and Play!

1 **Make** an animal bingo card.

2 **Play** Animal Bingo!

Lesson 8

1 🐝 **Spelling!** Complete.

1. d e _e_ r
2. f _ _ _
3. _ a t
4. h o _ _ e
5. r a _ b i _
6. d _ g

2 Complete and match.

1. _What_ is it?   It's a snake.

2. What _____ it?   It's a horse.

3. What is _____ ?   It's a rabbit.

4. _____ _____ _____ ?   It's an eagle.

3 **Word Play!** Find and circle the words from Unit 3 on Page 72.

UNIT 4 Lesson 1

1 Listen. Then echo.

doll

truck

kite

ball

yo-yo

teddy bear

2 Listen and circle.

Guess My Toy

I have a toy.
   Guess, guess, guess!

Is it a doll?
Yes, it is. / No, it isn't.

Is it a ball?
Yes, it is. / No, it isn't.

3 Page 13 **The Language Lodge**

32

Lesson 2

1 Sing:

Guess My Toy.

Is it a yo-yo?
Yes, it is. /
No, it isn't.

Is it a teddy bear?
Yes, it is. /
No, it isn't.

2 **Grammar Check!** **Complete.**

1. _____ it a ball?

   Yes, _____ _____ .

2. _____ _____ a yo-yo?

   No, _____ _____ .

3 **Point, ask, and answer.**

 Is it a doll?

 No, it isn't.

4 Page 14 **The Language Lodge**

Lesson 3

1   **Read and listen.**

1. It's the yo-yo contest!
2. Oh, no! Where's my yo-yo?
3. What color is it? Red? Black?
4. No, it isn't!

2 **Find and complete. Then listen and say.**

1. r e d
2. _ r e e n
3. _ e l l o w
4. _ l u e
5. _ l a c k
6. _ h i t e

3   **The Language Lodge**

Lesson 4

1 **Listen again to Happy Camp.**

2 Grammar Check! Unscramble.

1. it / is / color / What _____?

2. yellow / it / Is _____?

3. green / It's _____.

3 🐶 26 **Listen and cheer!**

What color is it?
It's green! It's green! It's green!

4 **The Language Lodge**

35

Lesson 5

1   **Read and listen.**

Trixie the Color Bear

Hi, I'm Trixie.
I love colors!
Look at the toys!

A green truck!
Splish, splash, splosh!
What color is it now?
It's red!

Splish, splash, splosh!
The ball isn't yellow now!
It's blue!

Look at the doll!
Is it blue now? No, it isn't!
It's yellow!

Colors are fun! Bye!

Lesson 6

1 🐶 27 **Listen again to Trixie the Color Bear.**

2 **Color before and after. Write the color after.**

1. It's red now.

2. _____.

3. _____.

3 **Answer.**

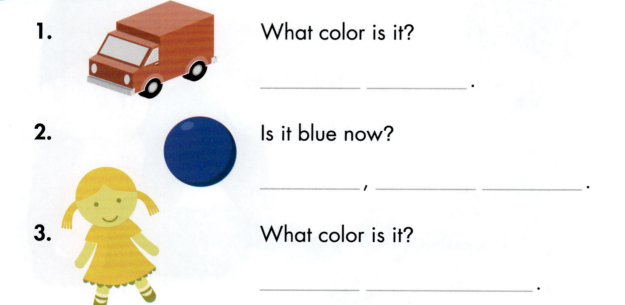

1. What color is it?

   _____ _____.

2. Is it blue now?

   _____, _____ _____.

3. What color is it?

   _____ _____.

Lesson 7
Make and Play!

1 Make a toy spinner.

2 Play Five Questions!

Is it a ball?
Yes, it is.
Is it black?
No, it isn't.

Lesson 8

1 🐝 Spelling! Match.

1. re   c k
2. y e l   e n
3. b l   l o w
4. b l a   d
5. g r e   u e

2 Circle.

1. It's red.

2. It's a doll.

3. It's green.

4. It's a yo-yo.

3 Word Play! Find and circle the words from Unit 4 on Page 72.

UNIT 5 Lesson 1

1 Listen. Then echo.

window

floor

table

chair

door

wall

2 Listen and check (✓).

Funny Places!

Open the door!
Look at that!
What is it?
It's a cat!

1.

3   The Language Lodge

Lesson 2

1 Sing: **Funny Places!**

2.

3.

2 Grammar Check! Complete.

1. The cat is _____ the table.

2. The cat is _____ the chair.

3. The cat is _____ the box.

3 Point and say.

 The cat is on the floor.

 The cat is on the wall.

4   **The Language Lodge**

41

Lesson 3

1   Read and listen.

2 Find and complete. Then listen and say.

1. m a p
2. wa __ er b __ tt __ e
3. __ n a c k
4. b a __ __ __ a c k
5. t __ w e l
6. h __ __ __

3   The Language Lodge

Lesson 4

1   **Listen again to Happy Camp.**

2 **Grammar Check! Match.**

1. Where's my water bottle?   It's on your head.
2. Where's my snack?   It's in your backpack.
3. Where's my backpack?   It's on the table.
4. Where's my hat?   It's on your bed.

3 **Listen and cheer!**

Where, where, where's my hat?
It's in your green backpack!

4   **The Language Lodge**

Lesson 5

1   **Read and listen.**

Where Is Getaway?

Mr. Marvel has a rabbit.
Whoosh!
The rabbit is in the hat!
Oh, no! Where is Getaway?
He's under the table!

Zoom!
Now Getaway is on the chair!
Getaway? Oh, no!
He's under the window.

Zip! Getaway is in the box!
Oh, no! He isn't in the box!
Where is Getaway?

He's in the truck!
Mr. Marvel is very sad.
And Getaway is very glad!

Lesson 6

1 🐶 33 **Listen again to Where Is Getaway?**

2 Circle.

1. Getaway is a cat.	Yes	(No)
2. Getaway is under the table.	Yes	No
3. Getaway is under the window.	Yes	No
4. Getaway is in the truck.	Yes	No
5. Getaway is sad.	Yes	No

3 Draw a new end to the story. Circle and answer.

Where is Getaway? He is in / on / under _____.

Lesson 7

Make and Play!

1 **Make** a mystery map.

2 **Play** Find It!

Where is your hat?
Is it in Blue 2?

Yes, it is!

Lesson 8

1 🐝 **Spelling!** Match.

1. un — dow
2. tab — or
3. flo — ir
4. back — der
5. win — pack
6. cha — le

2 Look, ask, and answer.

1. <u>Where's</u> the <u>backpack</u>?
   <u>It's</u> <u>on</u> <u>the</u> <u>table</u>.

2. _____ the yo-yo?
   _____ on _____.

3. Where's _____?
   It's _____.

4. _____?
   _____.

3 **Word Play!** Find and circle the words from Unit 5 on Page 72.

47

UNIT 6 Lesson 1

1 🐶 34 Listen. Then echo.

- tree
- plant
- butterfly
- caterpillar
- frog
- ladybug

2 🐶 35 Listen and number.

Nature Walk

What are they?
What? Where?
Look! Look! Look!
Over there!

☐ They're butterfl**ies**.

☐ They're ladybug**s**.

3 🏠 Page 21 The Language Lodge

Lesson 2

1 35 **Sing:**
Nature Walk.

☐ They're frogs.

1 They're trees.

2 **Grammar Check!** Complete.

1. What _____ they?

   _____ ladybugs.

2. _____ are _____ ?

   _____ butterflies.

3 **Point, ask, and answer.**

What are they?

They're butterflies.

4 Page 22 **The Language Lodge**

49

Lesson 3

1 36 **Read and listen.**

2 37 **Find and complete. Then listen and say.**

1. g r a y

2. p _ _ p _ e

3. o _ a _ g _

4. b _ o _ _

5. p _ _ _ _

6. b _ _ _ e

3 Page 23 **The Language Lodge**

50

Lesson 4

1 36 **Listen again to Happy Camp.**

Purple, beige, and orange!

Brown, pink, and gray, too!

3

They aren't red ladybugs. They're yellow!

Yes, they are.

What's that?

5

It's my frog!

4

2 **Grammar Check!** Circle.

1. Are they snakes?

2. No, they aren't.

3. They aren't red.

3 38 **Listen and cheer!**

Are they brown? No, they aren't.
They're purple! They're purple! Yes, they are!

CHEER BOX!

4 Page 24 **The Language Lodge**

51

Lesson 5

1   39 **Read and listen. Color.**

What are they?
They're brown eggs.
They're on the plant.

Look!
They're caterpillars.
They're yellow,
black, and white.

Are they caterpillars?
No, they aren't.
They're gray pupas.

Now, they're orange,
black, and white butterflies.
Hello, butterflies!

52

Lesson 6

1   **39** **Listen again to Hello, Butterflies!**

2 **Number.**

pupas

caterpillars

eggs

1

butterflies

3 **Read and draw.**

1. They're yellow, black, and white.

2. They're brown.

53

Lesson 7
Make and Play!

1 **Make** nature picture cards.

2 **Play** Ask Me!

Are they green?

54

Lesson 8

Round Up!

1 **Spelling! Complete.**

Nature

1. p l a n t s
2. f _ _ _ g _ _
3. b _ t _ e r _ _ i _ s
4. t r _ _ _ _ _
5. c _ _ t e _ _ ill _ r _

Colors

1. b e i g e
2. p _ r _ l _
3. g _ _ _ _ _
4. o r _ _ g _
5. p _ _ _ _ _

2 **Complete.**

1. Are they orange? Yes, _____.

2. Are they purple? No, _____.

3. Are they beige? _____, _____.

3 **Word Play! Find and circle the words from Unit 6 on Page 72.**

55

UNIT 7 — Lesson 1

1 **40** Listen. Then echo.

kitchen

living room

dining room

bedroom

bathroom

yard

2 **41** Listen and write the numbers.

My House

This is my house,
Come with me!
There are lots of rooms,
As you can see!

Downstairs, downstairs,
There is ___1___ kitchen!
There is _____ living room,
And _____ dining room, too!

Upstairs, upstairs,
There are _____ bedrooms.
Upstairs, upstairs,
There are _____ bathrooms, too!

3 Page 25 **The Language Lodge**

Lesson 2

1 41 Sing:

My House.

2 **Grammar Check!** Match.

kitchen.

There is — one — dining room.

three — living room.

There are — four — bedrooms.

bathrooms.

3 **Point and say.**

Dining room!

There is one dining room.

4 Page 26 **The Language Lodge**

57

Lesson 3

1 **42** Read and listen.

Wow! How many presents are there?

HAPPY BIRTHDAY

… eleven, twelve, thirteen. There are thirteen presents!

How many chairs are there?

… fifteen, sixteen, seventeen. There are seventeen chairs!

2 **43** Find and complete. Then listen and say.

11 e _____

12 t _____

13 t _____

14 f _____

15 f _____

16 s _____

17 s _____

18 e _____

19 n _____

20 t _____

3 Page 27 **The Language Lodge**

58

Lesson 4

1 🐶 `42` **Listen again to Happy Camp.**

How many balloons are there?

3

How many candles are there?

There are fourteen candles. Seven for Mia, and seven for Ali.

4

HAPPY BIRTHDAY

... eighteen, nineteen, twenty. There are twenty balloons!

Happy Birthday, Mia and Ali!

2 **Grammar Check!** **Write the questions.**

1. _How many presents are there_ ? There are 13.

2. _____ ? There are 17.

3. _____ ? There are 14.

4. _____ ? There are 20.

3 🐶 `44` **Listen and cheer!**

How many balloons are there?
There are twenty balloons!

CHEER BOX!

4 `Page 28` **The Language Lodge**

59

Lesson 5

1 🐶 45 **Read and listen.**

Different Homes

Look at this house.
It's very small. It has three rooms.
It has a kitchen and a bathroom.
The bedroom is also a living room in the day.

This house is a mansion.
There are many rooms.
There are fifteen bedrooms
and fifteen bathrooms!

There are many apartments here.
The apartments have two bedrooms.
There is one bathroom, a kitchen,
and a living room, too.

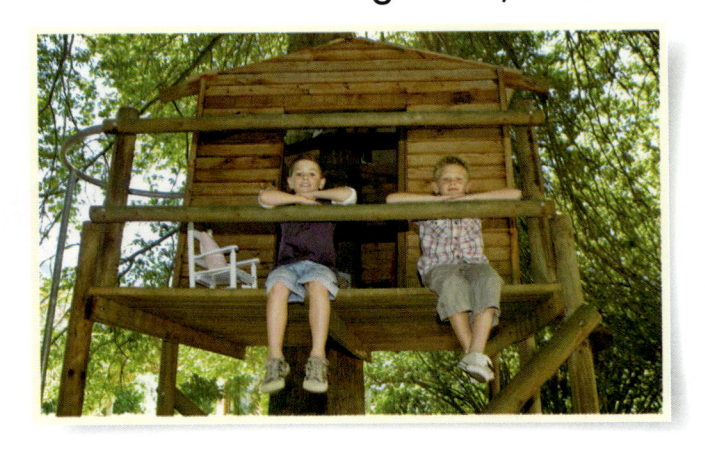

This is a tree house.
There is one room with two chairs.
It's a fun place to play!

60

Lesson 6

1 **45 Listen again to Different Homes.**

2 **Match.**

1. This is a fun place to play.

2. There are many rooms.

3. There is one room.

4. There are three rooms.

5. This home is very big.

6. There are two bedrooms.

7. This home is very small.

8. There are five rooms.

Lesson 7

Make and Play!

1 **Make** a mansion.

2 **Play** My Mansion!

How many kitchens are there?

There are eleven kitchens!

62

Lesson 8

Round Up!

1 🐝 **Spelling! Complete.**

1. y <u>a r</u> d

2. k _____ ch __ n

3. b a _____ o o __

4. t __ __ nt __

5. e l __ v __ __

6. s __ x __ __ e n

2 **Look and answer.**

1. How many bedrooms are there?

There <u>are</u> <u>three</u>.

2. How many kitchens are there?

_____ _____.

3. How many living rooms are there?

_____ _____.

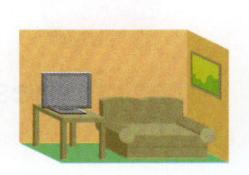

4. How many bathrooms are there?

_____ _____.

3 **Word Play!** Find and circle the words from Unit 7 on Page 72.

63

UNIT 8 Lesson 1

1 46

**Listen.
Then echo.**

hamburger

hot dog

pizza

French fries

milk

cookie

2 47 **Listen and circle.**

Lunchtime!

Lunchtime, lunchtime!
Munch, munch, munch.
What's on my tray
For my lunch?

I like pizza / milk,
For my lunch.
I like pizza / hamburgers,
Munch, munch, munch!

3 Page 29 **The Language Lodge**

64

Lesson 2

1 47 **Sing:**

Lunchtime!

I like French fries / hot dogs,
For my lunch.
I like cookies / hot dogs,
Munch, munch, munch!

2 **Grammar Check!** Complete.

1. ___I___ ___like___ pizza.

2. _____ _____ milk.

3. _____ _____ cookies.

3 **Point and say.**

I like cookies. I like hot dogs.

4 Page 30 **The Language Lodge**

Lesson 3

1 🐶 **48** **Read and listen.**

1 I don't like peas.

Leo, peas are good for you!

2 I don't like apples, bananas, or oranges.

Fruit is good for you.

2 🐶 **49** **Find and complete. Then listen and say.**

1. t o m a t o

2. p _____

3. a _____

4. c _____

5. b _____

6. o _____

3 🏠 Page 31 **The Language Lodge**

66

Lesson 4

1 48 **Listen again to Happy Camp.**

I like ice cream and cookies! Yummy!

3

Good, Cody! Tomatoes and carrots are good for you!

4

Ice cream and cookies aren't good for you!

Oh, no! I don't like tomatoes or carrots. They're for Iggy!

2 **Grammar Check!** Circle.

1. I like peas.
Yes   No

2. I don't like apples.
Yes   No

3. I don't like cookies.
Yes   No

4. I like carrots.
Yes   No

3 50 **Listen and cheer!**

I like carrots. I don't like peas.
Give me lots of carrots, please!

CHEER BOX!

4 Page 32 **The Language Lodge**

67

Lesson 5

1 **51 Read and listen.**

Lunchtime at the Zoo

It's lunchtime at the zoo.
Look at the monkey.
Monkeys like bananas a lot!

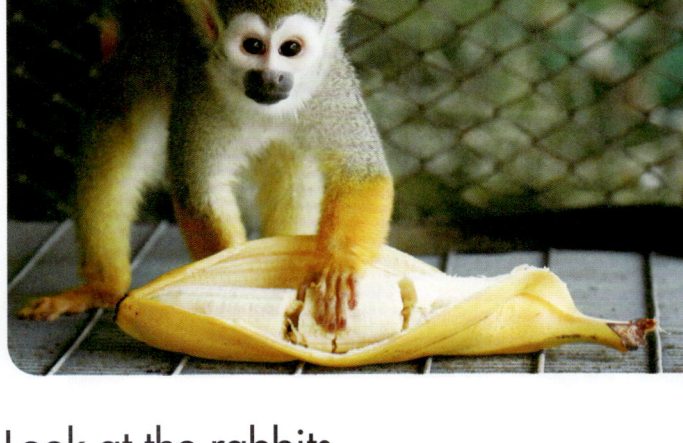

Look at the rabbits.
Rabbits eat fresh fruit and vegetables.
They like carrots and apples.
They don't like milk.

Horses like carrots and apples, too.
They don't like hamburgers or pizza!

Children like the zoo.
They also like hot dogs!

68

Lesson 6

1 51 Listen again to **Lunchtime at the Zoo**.

2 Complete.

like	bananas			hot dogs
don't like				

3 Match and say.

1. Monkeys like

2. Rabbits don't like

3. Horses don't like

4. Children like

69

Lesson 7
Make and Play!

1 **Make** food picture cards.

2 **Play** Lunchtime Memory!

Carrots!

I like carrots.

Lesson 8

Round Up!

1 🐝 Spelling! Complete.

1. p <u>i z z a</u>   2. a __ p __ e

3. c o __ __ i __   4. c __ r __ o __

5. o __ __ n g __   6. p __ a __

7. b __ n __ __ a   8. h __ __ b __ __ g __

2 Complete.

 1. I <u>like</u> hot dogs.

2. I _____ _____ carrots.

 3. I _____ cookies.

4. I _____ tomatoes.

5. I _____ pizza.

6. I _____ peas.

3 Word Play! Find and circle the words from Unit 8 on Page 72.

71

Word Play!

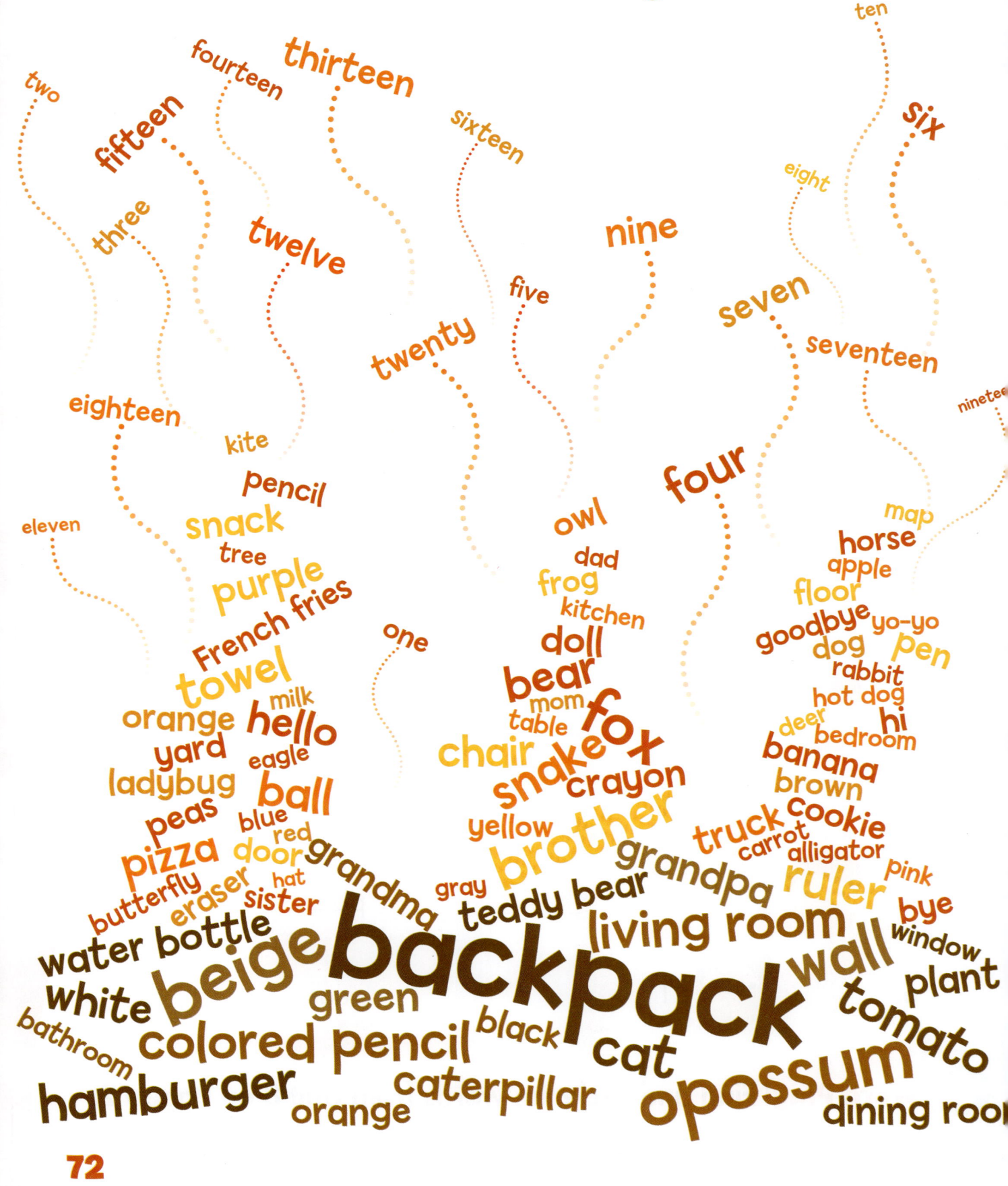

Lesson 4

✓ Grammar Check!

I **don't like** carrots.

❶ Circle.

1. (I like) / I don't like   tomatoes.

2. I like / I don't like   peas.

3. I like / I don't like   bananas.

4. I like / I don't like   carrots.

❷ Write about you.

1. I like ___pizza___ .

2. I don't like _____ .

3. _____ .

4. _____ .

Lesson 3

1 Write.

1.   tomatoes
2.   _____
3.   _____
4.   _____
5. _____
6. _____

2 Find and circle six food words.

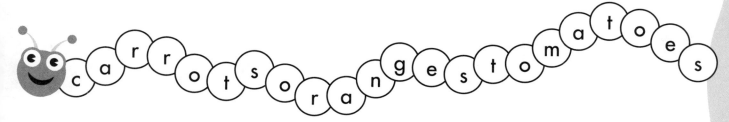

✓ **Vocabulary Check!** Cover, say, and check (✓).
I remember [1] [2] [3] [4] [5] [6] words.

Student Book **Page 66**

Lesson 2

Grammar Check!

I like hamburgers.

1 Choose and draw three things for your lunch.

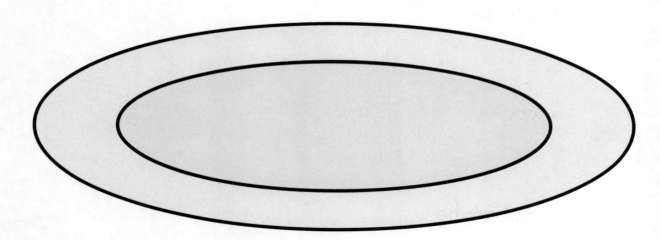

2 Write about your lunch.

1. I like _____ .

2. _____ .

3. _____ .

UNIT 8 Lesson 1

1 **Unscramble.**

1. crehnF rifse   F r e n c h   f r i e s

2. likm   _____

3. zapiz   _____

4. toh gdo   _____

5. oocike   _____

6. mahrgurbe   _____

✓ **Vocabulary Check!** Cover, say, and check (✓).

I remember [1] [2] [3] [4] [5] [6] words.

Student Book Page 64

Lesson 4

Grammar Check!

How many chairs are there?   There are three chairs.

1 Complete.

1. How many butterflies ___are___ ___there___ ?
   ___There___ ___are___ two butterflies___.

2. _____ _____ dogs _____ there?
   _____ _____ four _____ .

3. _____ _____ _____ are _____ ?
   _____ three _____ .

4. _____ _____ _____ _____ ?
   _____ eight _____ .

Lesson 3

1 Write the numbers.

1. eleven   _11_   2. fifteen   _____

3. thirteen _____   4. twenty   _____

2 Count and write the number words.

1. _fourteen_   2. _____   3. _____

4. _____   5. _____   6. _____

✓ **Vocabulary Check!** Cover, say, and check (✓).

I remember | 1 | 2 | 3 | 4 | 5 |
| 6 | 7 | 8 | 9 | 10 | words.

Lesson 2

✓ Grammar Check!

There is a yard.   There are four bedrooms.

1 Circle.

1. (There is) / There are a kitchen in the house.

2. There is / There are five crayons on the chair.

3. There is / There are two dogs in the living room.

4. There is / There are a hat on the table.

2 Read and draw.

1. There are four chairs in the kitchen.

2. There is a dog in the yard.

UNIT 7 Lesson 1

1 Label the rooms.

bathroom   bedroom   dining room
kitchen   living room   yard

dining room

✓ **Vocabulary Check!** Cover, say, and check (✓).

I remember ☐ 1 ☐ 2 ☐ 3 ☐ 4 ☐ 5 ☐ 6 words.

Student Book Page 56

Lesson 4

✓ Grammar Check!

Are they caterpillars?   No, they aren't.
They're frogs.

1 Circle.

1. Are they snakes? (Yes, they are.) / No, they aren't.

2. Are they frogs? Yes, they are. / No, they aren't.

3. Are they trees? Yes, they are. / No, they aren't.

4. Are they ladybugs? Yes, they are. / No, they aren't.

2 Complete. Write *They're* or *They aren't*.

1. _____ plants.
2. _____ butterflies.

Lesson 3

1 Read and color.

2 Find and circle six color words.

b	e	i	g	e	p
r	g	p	r	b	u
o	l	i	a	r	r
w	p	n	y	i	p
n	e	k	l	w	l
o	r	a	n	g	e

 Vocabulary Check! Cover, say, and check (✓).

I remember ☐1 ☐2 ☐3 ☐4 ☐5 ☐6 words.

Student Book **Page 50**

Lesson 2

✓ Grammar Check!

What are they?   They're trees.

1 Complete.

1. _____ are they?   _____ caterpillars.

2. _____ _____ they?   _____ plants.

3. _____ _____ _____ ?   _____ frogs.

2 Read and draw.

1. They're ladybugs.

2. They're butterflies.

22   Student Book **Page 49**

UNIT 6 Lesson 1

1 Complete.

1. t r e e

2. f __ o __

3. __ u t t __ __ f l __

4. __ a __ __ b __ g

5. p l __ __ __ __

6. c __ t __ r p __ ll __ r

✓ **Vocabulary Check!** Cover, say, and check (✓).

I remember ☐1 ☐2 ☐3 ☐4 ☐5 ☐6 words.

Student Book Page 48

Lesson 4

✓ Grammar Check!

Where's the snack?   It's on the floor.

1 Look and answer.

1. Where's the water bottle?
   It's on the table.

2. Where's the hat?
   _____.

3. Where's the towel?
   _____.

4. Where's the map?
   _____.

Lesson 3

1 Circle.

1. water bottle

2. towel

3. snack

4. hat

5. map

6. backpack

✓ **Vocabulary Check!** Cover, say, and check (✓).

I remember ☐1 ☐2 ☐3 ☐4 ☐5 ☐6 words.

Student Book **Page 42**

Lesson 2

✓ Grammar Check!

The cat is in / on / under the box.

❶ Circle.

1. The crayon is in / on / under the pencil case.

2. The pencil is in / on / under the floor.

3. The ruler is in / on / under the table.

❷ Read and draw.

1. The pen is under the table.

2. The ball is on the chair.

UNIT 5 Lesson 1

1 Complete.

1. w <u>a l l</u>
2. d ___ o ___
3. f ___ ___ r
4. t ___ ___ e
5. c ___ ___ r
6. w ___ ___ w

✓ **Vocabulary Check!** Cover, say, and check (✓).

I remember [1] [2] [3] [4] [5] [6] words.

Lesson 4

Grammar Check!

What color is it?   It's red.

1 **Complete.**

1. What ___color___ is it?   It's bl _a_ _c_ k.

2. _____ color is it?   It's r e ___ and w h _____ e.

3. What color _____ _____ ?   _____ y _____ o w.

4. _____ _____ _____ it?   _____ b _____ e.

2 **Color. Unscramble and answer.**

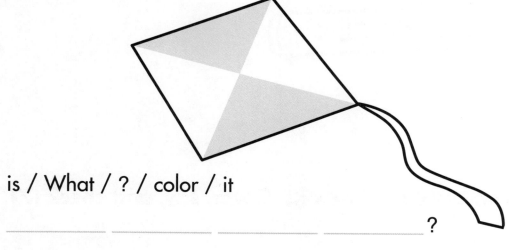

is / What / ? / color / it

_____ _____ _____ _____ ?

It's _____ .

Lesson 3

1 Read and color. Then write.

1. BLUE — It's   blue .
2. WHITE — _____ .
3. RED — _____ .
4. BLACK — _____ .
5. YELLOW — _____ .
6. GREEN — _____ .

✓ **Vocabulary Check!** Cover, say, and check (✓).

I remember 1 2 3 4 5 6 words.

Lesson 2

✓ Grammar Check!

Is it a doll?   Yes, it is.   No, it isn't.

1 Circle.

1. Is it a teddy bear?   Yes, it is.   No, it isn't.

2. Is it a ball?   Yes, it is.   No, it isn't.

3. Is it a truck?   Yes, it is.   No, it isn't.

4. Is it a doll?   Yes, it is.   No, it isn't.

2 Read and draw.

1. Is it a yo-yo?
   No, it isn't. It's a ball.

2. Is it a teddy bear?
   Yes, it is.

UNIT 4   Lesson 1

1 Find and circle six toys.

t	e	d	d	y	b	e	a	r
r	m	a	s	o	a	x	l	k
u	j	g	r	y	l	w	b	m
c	k	q	p	o	l	r	b	k
k	i	t	e	g	d	o	l	l

2 Complete.

1. It's a ___Kite___.

2. It's a _____.

3. It's a _____.

4. It's a _____.

 Vocabulary Check! Cover, say, and check (✓).

I remember | 1 | 2 | 3 | 4 | 5 | 6 | words.

Student Book **Page 32**

Lesson 4

✓ Grammar Check!

It's a bear.   It isn't an owl.

1 Circle.

1. (It's) / It isn't a cat.   2. It's / It isn't a horse.

3. It's / It isn't a fox.   4. It's / It isn't a rabbit.

2 Complete.

1. _____ an eagle.

2. _____ _____ a bear.

3. _____ a deer.

Lesson 3

1 Unscramble.

1. xof   f o x

2. legae   _ _ _ _ _

3. rabe   _ _ _ _ _

4. wol   _ _ _ _

5. eder   _ _ _ _

6. kanes   _ _ _ _ _

✓ **Vocabulary Check!** Cover, say, and check (✓).
I remember 1 2 3 4 5 6 words.

Lesson 2

✓ Grammar Check!

What is it?   It's a cat.   It's an alligator.

1 Circle *a* or *an*.

1. It's a / (an) opossum.

2. It's a / an dog.

3. It's a / an alligator.

4. It's a / an rabbit.

2 Complete.

1. What _____ it?   It's _____ horse.

2. What _____ _____ ?   It's _____ opossum.

3. _____ _____ _____ ?   It's _____ cat.

UNIT 3 Lesson 1

1 Complete.

1. h <u>o</u> <u>r</u> <u>s</u> e

2. r _____ b _____ _____

3. a _____ l _____ _____ t _____ r

4. _____ _____ g

5. o _____ _____ s s _____

6. c _____ _____

✓ **Vocabulary Check!** Cover, say, and check (✓).

I remember | 1 | 2 | 3 | 4 | 5 | 6 | words.

 Student Book Page 24

Lesson 4

✓ Grammar Check!

I have a pencil.   I have an eraser.

1 Match.

1. I have an eraser.   2. I have a crayon.   3. I have a ruler.

2 Complete.

1. I have _a_   ✏️ .

2. I _____ a 🖊️ .

3. I have _____ 🧽 .

Lesson 3

1 Circle.

1. pen

2. eraser

3. crayon

4. colored pencil

5. pencil

6. ruler

✓ **Vocabulary Check!** Cover, say, and check (✓).

I remember ☐1 ☐2 ☐3 ☐4 ☐5 ☐6 words.

Student Book **Page 18**

Lesson 2

✓ Grammar Check!

How old are you?   I'm ten.

1 Draw the candles on your cake.

2 Answer.

How old are you?

I'm _____ !

UNIT 2   Lesson 1

1 Complete and match.

___ i v e 1

___ e n 2

___ i x 3

_o_ n e 4

___ i g h t 5

___ w o 6

___ i n e 7

___ e v e n 8

___ h r e e 9

___ o u r 10

✓ **Vocabulary Check!** Cover, say, and check (✓).

I remember ☐1 ☐2 ☐3 ☐4 ☐5

☐6 ☐7 ☐8 ☐9 ☐10 words.

Student Book Page 16

Lesson 4

✓ **Grammar Check!**

This is my grandpa.

1 Draw and complete.

1. This is my _____.

2. This is my _____.

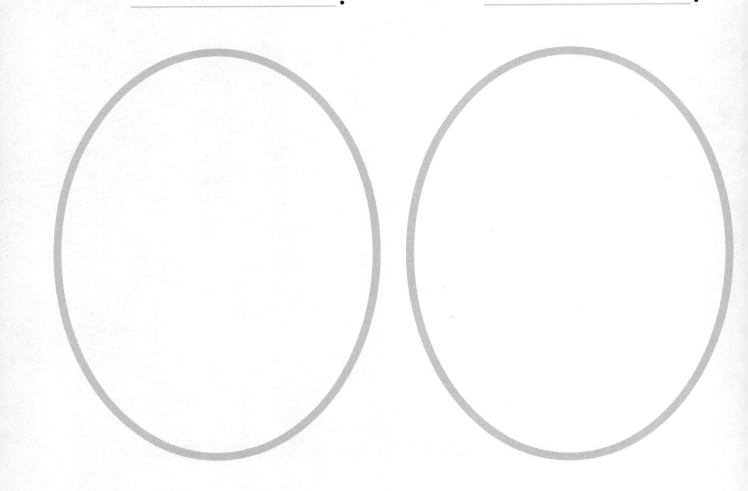

Lesson 3

1 Match.

1. grandma
2. dad
3. brother
4. mom
5. sister
6. grandpa

2 Complete.

♀	♂
1. g r a n d m a	4. _ r _ _ d p _
2. m _ _	5. d _ d
3. _ is _ er	6. b _ t _ e _

✓ **Vocabulary Check!** Cover, say, and check (✓).

I remember ☐1 ☐2 ☐3 ☐4 ☐5 ☐6 words.

Student Book Page 10

Lesson 2

✓ **Grammar Check!**

What's your name?   My name's Bob.

1 Answer the question. Draw a picture of you.

What's your name?

My _____ .

UNIT 1 Lesson 1

1 Look and write.

Hi   Bye
Goodbye   Hello

H e l l o !

___ i !

___ y ___ !

___ o o d b ___ e !

✓ **Vocabulary Check!** Cover, say, and check (✓).
I remember 1 2 3 4 words.